Although we look different, we really are the same.
Your features are beautiful, so don't be ashamed.
You are our baby, our pride, and our joy.
We love you so much because you are our little boy.
No matter if you're mixed with purple, orange,
or any other color, I will love you forever,
because I am your mother.

To Jarrett, Bobby, Mica, and Chet with love.

No part of this book may be reproduced, transmitted, or sold in an information retrieval system in any form or by any means, graphic, electronic, or mechanical, including photocopying, typing and recording, without prior written permission from the publisher.

Text Copyright © 2012 by Gina Golliday-Cabell
Illustrations Copyright © 2012 by Create Space
ISBN: 1469983168
ISBN-13: 978-1469983165
Printed in the United States of America
All rights reserved.
Library of Congress Control Number: 2012902018
CreateSpace Independent Publishing Platform, North Charleston, SC

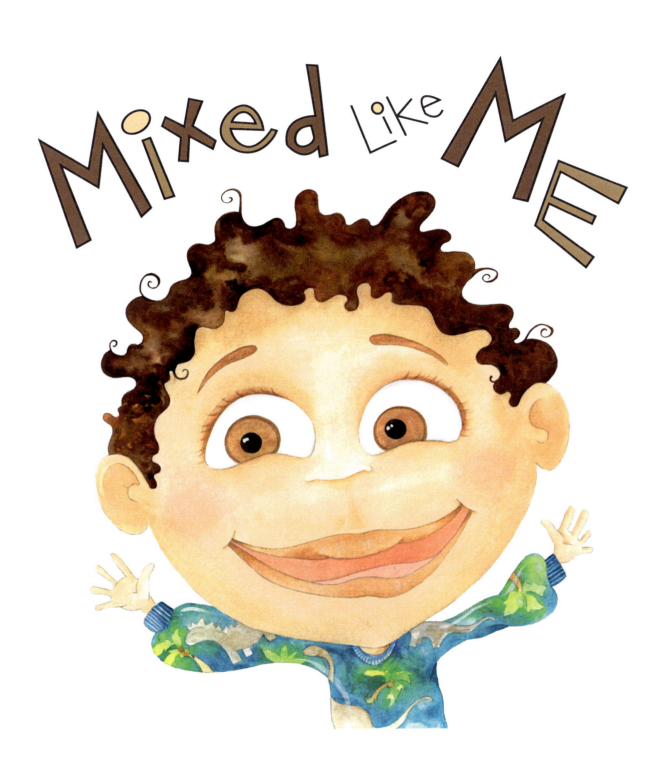

Mixed Like ME

by

Gina Golliday-Cabell

Mommy, why are you not mixed like me?
You look like vanilla with honey from a bee.
And Daddy looks like chocolate milk
that's smooth and creamy just like silk.
But still, no one is mixed like me.
I don't think I fit in.
Can't you see?

My eyes are tan; they look just like sand.
Your eyes are green; they look just like a jelly bean.
Daddy's eyes are black, like the magic man's hat.
I don't understand. Was it supposed to happen like that?
Why can't you both be mixed like me?
I don't want to be mixed.
Can't you see?

It just isn't fair.
I really don't like this curly hair.
Why can't it be straight, or spongy like cake?
If I weren't mixed, it would be so great!

Do I have to be mixed?
Mommy, take this mix out of me!
I really don't like being mixed like me.

Sweetheart, I love you, because you are YOU!
Take that frown off your face, and don't look so blue.
I'm proud of your mixture. It came from Daddy and me.
You turned out perfectly!
Can't you see?

Thank you, Mommy! I think I understand!
It's great to be mixed, and you're my biggest fan!
We both have two eyes, two ears, two legs,
and two hands.
But you are a girl, and I am a little man!

That's right!

It doesn't matter what mixture you are,
or if you come from lands near or far.
As long as we respect and love one another,
in God's eyes we are all sisters and brothers.

Now let me tuck you in so that you can sleep tight.
I really can't let you stay up all night!

Mommy, I'm so happy to be mixed like me,
and I know you think I'm cute as a pea!

Goodnight, sweetheart.
I love you.

Made in United States
North Haven, CT
25 May 2022